We were there

THE
1940s

Rosemary Rees

Heinemann Library,
an imprint of Heinemann Publishers (Oxford) Ltd,
Halley Court, Jordan Hill, Oxford, OX2 8EJ

OXFORD LONDON EDINBURGH
MADRID PARIS ATHENS BOLOGNA
MELBOURNE SYDNEY AUCKLAND
SINGAPORE TOKYO IBADAN
NAIROBI GABORONE HARARE
PORTSMOUTH NH (USA)

© Heinemann Library 1993

First published 1993
93 94 95 96 10 9 8 7 6 5 4 3 2 1

British Library Cataloguing in Publication Data
is available on request from the British Library.

ISBN 0 431 07329 5

Designed by Philip Parkhouse
Printed and bound in China

Acknowledgements
The author and publisher would like to thank the following
for permission to reproduce photographs:
Hulton Picture Company: pp. 5, 6, 7, 8, 9, 10, 11, 13, 15,
16, 17, 19, 20, 21, 23, 25, 28, 30,
Imperial War Museum: p. 26
Magnum Photos/George Rodger: pp. 4, 14, 22
Popperfoto: p. 24; Topham: pp. 12, 18, 27
Cover photograph: Hulton Picture Company

The author and publisher would like to thank all of the people who
contributed memories for this book.

> ## Note to the reader
> In this book there are some words in the text
> which are printed in **bold type**. This shows that
> the words are listed in the glossary on page 31.
> The glossary gives a brief explanation of words
> that may be new to you.

Contents

Home 1

There was a war between Britain and Germany. This man's house was bombed by German planes in 1940.

Geoff Bown, when he was a boy in Gidea Park, Essex.

One month there were air raids every night. German planes flew over Essex and dropped bombs on houses and railway stations, factories and oil refineries. One night I was woken up by two terrible crashes. In the morning we found out that our parish church and a nearby house had been destroyed and lots of other houses badly damaged.

I was a Cub Scout, so I put on my uniform and went to help. I spent the day with other Cubs and Scouts helping to sort out people's belongings from their shattered homes. One of our Scouts lived in the house that had been destroyed. He was away that night, but as soon as he heard what had happened, he went home. He helped the rescue workers to dig through the rubble and rescued his mother and younger sister from the ruins. He was given the Scout gallantry medal for being so brave.

Geoff Bown, when he was a boy living in Gidea Park, Essex.

My parents took me by train to a town in Hampshire where an uncle lived. They left me there. I had been **evacuated**! I didn't mind much because I had been to Uncle's house before, and I knew he could be fun. But there was a whole new world before me. The house was modern and had a huge garden with a grass tennis court. All round there was nothing to see but fields. My Uncle and Auntie lived there with my cousin Mary. A lot of people were staying with them. There was Winnie (another cousin) who had been evacuated from west London. There were Peter, Angela and their mother (whom I did not know) who had been evacuated from south-east London. There was Uncle's secretary, too. She helped Uncle with his work. I was the youngest person in the whole house. At home I had no brothers or sisters, and found it strange to be living with lots of people.

This little boy was saying goodbye to his father. He was going with other children to stay in the country where they would be safe.

Home 2

These people were putting Anderson shelters in their back gardens. The shelters kept them safe when the bombs began to fall.

Elisabeth Bown, who was a girl living in Romford, Essex.
One night in May 1941 the air raids were really bad and we decided to sleep in our shelter. Our tabby cat had just had three kittens. They were all sleeping in a cardboard box by the boiler. My dad was worried about them and so he took the box and the kittens into the shelter with us. The cat didn't like this at all. She picked them all up, one at a time, by the scruff of the neck, and carried them into the front room of our house. We wondered why she had not taken them back to the warm boiler in the back kitchen. There was nothing we could do because just then the bombs began to fall. A few minutes later there was a dreadful explosion: a land mine had fallen half a mile away.

The tiles on our back roof blew off and all the windows at the back of our house were blown in and broken. The kitchen was covered in broken glass, but our cat and her kittens were safe in the front room.

Rosemary Dawson, who was a girl living in Pinner, about twenty miles from London.

I was three and a half when the war ended in 1945. Even though I was very young, I can remember that my mother and father had an allotment. This was a piece of land the other side of our garden where they grew vegetables. They grew potatoes, cabbages, runner beans, parsnips, carrots, brussel sprouts and peas. They grew tomatoes and lettuces, radishes and cucumbers.

Sometimes my grandpa came over to help with the digging. Sometimes I was allowed to take my watering can and water the growing plants. Of course all the vegetables were ready to eat at the same time. We couldn't possibly eat them all at once, and there were no such things as freezers which would freeze the vegetables and so keep them fresh for a long time. My mother had to spend hours bottling vegetables and fruit in large glass **Kilner jars** for us to eat in the winter months ahead.

During the war there was not enough food in the shops. This family had grown a lot of vegetables in their garden.

Home 3

During the war everyone had a ration book which said how much food they could buy.

Con Dawson, who was a young housewife living in Pinner, about twenty miles from London.

The government decided to ration some important food early on in the war. They rationed sugar, eggs, butter, cheese, meat, bacon, milk, sweets, tea and soap. How much you were allowed depended on supplies. Some people were allowed more than others. When I was pregnant I had a special green ration book. This meant that I got first choice of any fruit the greengrocer had in, and twice the egg ration. When my daughter, Rosemary, was born she had a blue ration book. This meant she could have fresh fruit when there was any, and an extra half pint of milk a week. Sometimes rumours would go round that the butcher had some extra meat, or there had been a surprise delivery of bananas to the greengrocer. We all rushed to the shops and queued for hours to try and buy something extra for our families.

Women spent a lot of time queuing for food. They spent a lot of time, too, making sure their families were clean and healthy.

Janet Withersby, when she was a child living in Liverpool.

Mondays were wash days. First my mother sorted the washing. Sheets, pillow cases, tablecloths and my father's collars were put into one pile. Later in the day a horse-drawn laundry van came to collect them. Then my mother lit the gas boiler. When the water was boiling she washed all the towels and my little sister's nappies. She put them through the **mangle** and hung them out to dry. Mother next poured very hot water into a tub and added soap powder. She put the clothes in and swooshed them up and down with a posser, which was a long wooden stick with a metal bowl fixed on one end. When the clothes were clean, she rinsed them, put them through the mangle and hung them up to dry.

Wash day was very steamy and there were puddles on the scullery floor. My sister howled in her playpen all morning. I had to stay on my chair and finish a very hard jigsaw.

School 1

This photograph was taken in 1941 during an air raid. These school children were having their lessons in an air raid shelter.

Peggy George, when she was a girl living in Caerphilly, south Wales.

I began secondary school at the Caerphilly Grammar School in September 1943. It was an all-girls school. Because of the war there were brick walls around the ground floor of the school and the windows were criss-crossed with strips of tape. This was to protect us from the blast if any bombs fell. We were only seven miles from Cardiff and the docks there were

bombed often. Only a few stray bombs fell in Caerphilly, but not when I was in school.

I remember I did not like maths and science, and I especially hated chemistry. The laboratory was cold and full of awful smells. Although the school was so near to Caerphilly castle we were never taught anything about it. This was odd because its famous leaning tower was part of our school badge which was on my green school blazer and **beret**.

Reg George, when he was a boy living in Barry, south Wales.

Our parents had to pay if we went to grammar school. The day before the start of term was spent queuing to pay the fee of £2 10s 0d. This was more than my father earned in a week, so finding the money caused problems. At least the books were free!

Each day I took my satchel, full of books, to school. I also took my gas mask in a cardboard box, just in case the Germans dropped gas bombs.

The older boys were fire-watchers. Every night a group of them stayed in school. They were on watch in case a fire bomb dropped on the school. This did happen one night, and the roof caught fire. The boys put the fire out. One day when I was walking home from school the sirens sounded. We looked up and saw a **Spitfire** shoot down a German plane. We all cheered! In June 1945 we had a special assembly because the war in Europe was over. That was a great day!

This photograph was taken during the war. The teacher was making sure the boy's gas mask fit properly.

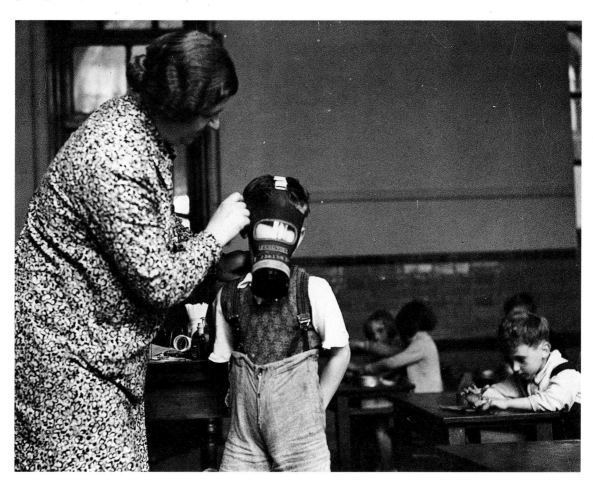

School 2

These children were waiting to board a train. They were being evacuated to the countryside.

Geoff Bown, who was a boy during the war, remembers what it was like to be evacuated and to have to go to a new school.

The local primary school couldn't cope with all the extra children. Because I was an **evacuee** I could only go to school in the mornings. We had a fierce elderly lady teacher. She made us say the Lord's Prayer and the Ten Commandments. We learned to leave the school as soon as the air raid siren sounded. We walked down the road to a builders' warehouse. There we sat amongst manhole covers, basins and pipes while our teachers tried to carry on with our lessons. It didn't really work and soon we were moved to the Bethel chapel. Workmen started building air raid shelters for us in the school playground. Once or twice the siren didn't sound, and I remember watching with the workmen as British and German planes fought in the skies above us.

This photograph was taken in May 1940, at a school in Yorkshire. The boys were knitting scarves for soldiers.

Janet Withersby remembers what it was like to start school in 1948, after the war was over.

I started infant school in 1948. My mother took me to school for the first few weeks. After that I took myself to school. I was allowed to go on the bus when it rained. Otherwise I walked. When I was a junior I called for my friends, but when I was little I didn't know where they lived.

In the playground we played fairies and witches, which was a kind of '**tig**'.

We girls also played rhyme games like 'Bell horses, bell horses, what time of day' and singing games like 'In and out those darky bluebells'. We played dipping games like 'Dip, dip, dip, my blue ship'. Groups of children often walked around in a long row with arms around each other's necks chanting rhymes and sayings. Our favourite was "We won the war!" We infants did not remember the war and did not know what we were chanting about. It was just a playground habit.

Work 1

Bombs have landed on these houses. There might be people buried in the rubble. The men are working hard to find them.

Mrs E. Gilbert remembers what it was like to work in the women's Auxiliary Territorial Service (ATS).

I started my service life at Pontefract Barracks in December 1943. We did our initial training to knock us into shape for army life. We were kitted out with our uniform, including underwear and PT kit, given a number and pay book. Our pay was ten shillings a week and we had to salute our paymaster for that.

I gained a special operator's badge, and was posted to Kent. We worked with the Intelligence Corps of the army in an underground unit. Our work was secret and we weren't allowed to talk about it. We **intercepted** messages in code from the enemy in Germany. The intelligence Unit **decoded** them. I was on duty when the last message came through from the enemy. It was 'The Tommy's are coming!' 'Tommy' was the nickname for a British soldier. We knew then that the war was over.

These women were working in the open air because their office was destroyed by bombs. Most people were luckier than this.

Rita Mann, who lived in West Hartlepool, Co Durham, remembers her first job.

In 1945, when I was fourteen years old, I started work at Marks and Spencer. The war was not over properly, and people were still working in war time jobs. This meant that the store couldn't find anybody to work as cleaners. Another girl and I had to scrub the doorsteps before the shop opened. It opened at 8.50am Mondays to Saturday, and closed at 5.30pm every day except Wednesday, when it closed at 1.00pm and Saturdays when closing time was 6.00pm. On Saturdays we had to stay late to scrub the food counters and count the clothing coupons people had given us from their ration books. I was paid £1 4s 6d a week. I gave £1 to my mother and kept the 4s 6d for myself. My mother bought my clothes and gave me dinner money and bus fares to work. After work my friends and I went dancing, roller skating or to the cinema.

Work 2

During the war, women took over a lot of jobs which men did before they went to fight. This woman was using a machine to make guns.

Frank Williams remembers what it was like to be in the navy during the war.

Leaving the wife and children behind was hard. They knew my ship might be sunk by the enemy and I might not come back. I knew they might be bombed out and killed or injured while I was away at sea, and I wouldn't be able to help. I probably wouldn't even know until I got home and found there wasn't a home there at all.

All sailors felt the same, but once we were on the ship we concentrated on the work we had to do. We sailed in convoys across the Atlantic, protecting merchant ships bringing food and other goods to Britain. We were hunted by German submarines and managed to sink two before we were **holed** just below the waterline.

The worst convoys were to Russia. The sea froze as the waves crashed on deck. I always wore gloves. If you touched metal with your bare hands, the skin and flesh would stick to it.

During the war the Women's Land Army took over a lot of job on farms. These women were ploughing on a farm in Monmouthshire.

Kay Styles remembers what it was like to work as an actress at the end of the war.

I trained at Drama School for three years, and then I joined a **repertory** company. Every city and most towns had their own repertory company of actors and actresses. They put on plays and shows for the people who lived in the town.

Our company put on a new play every week. On Tuesday mornings we met and read through the new play.

We only had a week to learn our lines for the new play, and at the same time, we were acting the old one in the evenings. It could get very confusing.

I was paid £8 a week and had to buy all the clothes I needed for acting on the stage, as well as the clothes I wanted to wear when I was not acting.

There was very little life outside the theatre, but we all loved our work. We all had our fans who brought us chocolate, bars of soap or flowers.

Spare Time 1

These boys were pretending to be soldiers. One had his gas mask with him, in a box, in case there was a real gas attack.

Rosemary Dawson, when she was a girl living in Pinner, twenty miles from London.
It was difficult for parents to get hold of toys during the war. The factories were busy turning out guns and **shells**. So a lot of toys were home made, or passed on to younger children when the older ones had grown out of them. However, I didn't in any way feel hard done by.

My favourite toy was a clockwork trainset which my parents bought from a neighbour. The engine was green. You had to hold the wheels when you wound it up, and then put it down very carefully on the metal rails, letting go of the back wheels at the same time. The rails made a big circle. Later on I had points, a signal box and a signal.

I had one very special doll. She was dressed as a Russian peasant. All her clothes came off: dress, petticoats and knickers. I called her Anna and I still have her.

Peter Carpenter was evacuated from West Yorkshire, to North Yorkshire during the war.
Father was a dentist in Bradford, and home was a large house with a live-in maid and a garden with a grass tennis court. In Settle I had to live with the local butcher and his two sons.

I had a marvellous time. When we came back from school we had to help sweep out the shop and scrub the enormous wooden chopping block. Then we had tea. There was always plenty to eat, and if we were still hungry at the end, we filled up with vast slices of bread and jam. This was very different from mother's tea parties! Instead of a garden to play in, I roamed with the other boys over the **fells and moors**. I learned to snare rabbits and catch trout in the local river. One Sunday morning we **dammed** up the stream that ran by a local churchyard. The church flooded before morning service. We were caught and beaten, and we deserved it!

These children lived in cities. Cities were dangerous places during the war because of the bombs. These children were sent to the countryside to keep them safe.

Spare Time 2

This little girl was sitting in the window of a bombed out shop in London. She was drawing a picture.

Sallie Cooper, when she was a girl living in Mill Hill, London.

Sweets were rationed, and toys and books were **scarce** and expensive. Sometimes we had ice cream, but it was usually only as a birthday treat. My father made me a doll's house. It had electric lights which ran off a battery. He made me a farmyard and a garden swing.

I spent my pocket money on comics and lead farm animals whose legs were always breaking off. My best friend and I pushed our scooters along the pavements and raced downhill on roller skates.

When I was seven I joined the Brownies. I wore a brown tunic and a brown woollen hat. I danced around a wooden toadstool singing 'We are the Little People, tall and straight as any steeple'. At home we played cards, ludo, **halma** and chess. Every day, I listened to Children's Hour on the **wireless**.

These girls were called the 'Sunbeam Four'. They gave concerts to friends and neighbours during the war.

Peggy George, when she was a girl in Caerphilly, south Wales.

During the war years we used to go to the cinema on Saturday night. There were always long queues to get in. My father estimated the length of the queue, and was a good judge of whether we would get in or not. Sometimes when my father bought the tickets, the woman in the **box office** would give him the tickets and three sheets of newspaper. This meant that all the seats were taken and we had to sit on the steps in the balcony. Nobody seemed to think it strange.

We went to the cinema in the Rhondda one night in 1941. I was with my aunt and two cousins, and we saw Shirley Temple in a film called 'Blue Bird'. I was very excited because it was the first colour film I had ever seen. When we came out, the sky was lit up with **flares** and we could hear bombs dropping. My aunt made us crouch against the wall of the Workmans' Hall. I could feel the wall shake.

Spare Time 3

These people were in an air raid shelter. They tried to have fun and pass the time while the bombs fell.

Reg George, when he was a boy in south Wales.

Every evening special black curtains were pulled across the windows. We all had to have them. No **chink** of light had to show. The authorities were afraid that German bombers would see the lights of towns and drop bombs on them.

We kept cheerful by playing ludo and snakes and ladders. Best of all, though, was the wireless. I especially enjoyed Tommy Handley and the characters in his show: Mrs Mopp and Funf the German spy.

Most nights we listened to 'Lord Haw-Haw'. His real name was William Joyce. He broadcast from Germany and tried to scare us by saying which streets were going to be bombed next. He frightened a lot of people. One night he mentioned streets in our town. Nothing happened, and we all laughed even more at him the next night.

**This photograph was taken in Plymouth in July 1941.
Even though there was a war on, some people
managed to enjoy themselves!**

**Karen Lancaster remembers what
it was like to be young just after
the war.**

I lived in Porthcawl, a seaside town in
south Wales, until I was eight years
old. We played outside most of the
time, and rode our tricycles around the
streets. There was not much traffic and
it was very safe. When I was older I
was allowed to have a pair of roller
skates. I especially liked scrambling
over the huge rocks in Rest Bay looking
for crabs, star fish and **sea anemones**.

Every Sunday I went to chapel, with
my mother and elder brother.
Everyone there spoke Welsh.

My father was away fighting in the
war. My brother and I, and two other
children were the only Welsh speaking
children in Porthcawl. Every Sunday
we learned a verse from the bible and
had to say it to all the congregation.
When I was very small I had to learn
'Da yw Duw', which means 'God is
good'. The verses got longer as we
got older!

Holidays 1

Mrs Richard, who lived in Liskeard, Cornwall, looked after 12 evacuee children. Here some of them helped make a Christmas cake.

Rosemary Dawson remembers Christmas just after the war when she was four years old.

We had a real Christmas tree. It had roots and was going to be planted in the garden afterwards. It stood in a pot in the lounge and I was allowed to help decorate it. My job was to put white cotton wool carefully along all the main branches. It was supposed to look like snow. It took me a long time because the cotton wool kept falling off. When I had finished, I sprinkled glitter over the cotton wool to make it sparkle.

My mother hung decorations from the branches, and my father made sure the lights worked. These were coloured bulbs strung along a twisty **flex** and plugged in to the electricity. Each bulb screwed into a little brown connector on the flex. If one bulb was faulty, none of them would work. It took a long time to find out which bulb (or bulbs) wouldn't work, and replace them.

These girls could not play on the beach. During the war, mines were buried on some beaches in case the Germans invaded.

Elisabeth Bown remembers a day at the seaside during the war when she was seven years old.
During the war you could only go to the seaside at a few places. This was because most beaches were **mined** and covered in barbed wire. One day my Dad took me by train to Chalkwell, near Southend-on-Sea. The beach was crowded because it was a nice, sunny day. We had a paddle in the sea and then ate our corned beef and margarine sandwiches. Dad said he would see if he could find a cup of tea, and told me to stay where I was until he came back. Suddenly the air raid sirens sounded, and everyone ran from the beach. They were afraid of being machine gunned by enemy planes. I didn't know where my Dad was, so I sat where he'd told me to stay. I was the only person on the beach. Dad came back as quickly as he could. He was very pleased that I had done what I had been told, otherwise I would have been lost. I felt very brave.

Holidays 2

lend a hand on the land

at a farming holiday camp

During the war the government issued posters to try to get people to help on farms.

Frank Wheeldon went on a wartime farm holiday with his wife, Kitty.

Kitty and I were married during the war. I worked in an **iron foundry** and so I didn't have to join the armed forces. We decided to try one of the farm holidays the government were always advertising. It seemed a good way of helping the country's war effort and getting a bit of a holiday at the same time.

We went to a farm in Devon – and it was very hard work! The men who were on holiday helped get in the harvest of wheat. These were the days before combine harvesters, and we had to bang the sheaves of wheat together to make **stooks**. When all the wheat was dry, we **pitchforked** it into wagons so that it could be taken away to be threshed.

The women worked in the cowshed and dairy, milking the cows and making butter, cream and cheese. It certainly wasn't a holiday - but the food was marvellous!

Janet Withersby, when she was a child just after the war.

We used to go on holiday to my grandparents' house in Sunderland. Before we went my mother washed, ironed, packed and worried about clothes getting creased. My father sent some of our luggage by train about a week before we were due to go away. He arranged to collect it from the station in Sunderland after we arrived there.

The night before setting off I used to walk with my father to our local police station. He arranged for a policeman to keep an eye on our house while we were away, just in case burglars decided to break in.

On the day of our journey we packed some of the luggage in the bottom of our big pram. With my little sister on top, we pushed the pram to the station. It was going to travel in the guard's van. Our holiday trains always seemed full of cheerful soldiers and airmen, carrying their kit bags.

Between June and October 1942, 600 boys and girls from London schools went to help on farms owned by the education authority.

Special Days 1

This is a photograph of a wartime wedding at Islington register office in London.

Frank Wheeldon remembers his wedding to Kitty during the war.

Kitty and I very nearly didn't get married at all. The first day we decided on was January 22nd. I worked in an iron foundry, and was able to arrange for a week's holiday at that time. Kitty, however, was in the women's Auxiliary Territorial Service. She was trained to decode messages from the enemy, and could be sent anywhere in the country. Because she had signed the Official Secrets Act, she couldn't tell me where she was going, what she was doing, or when she would be going. On January 21 she was sent to Shropshire, and the wedding was cancelled. This happened twice more, and my mother was beginning to think that Kitty didn't really want to marry me. Finally, in June, she was given Special Leave for one day. It was all arranged so quickly that only our parents and a couple of cousins could come to celebrate with us. We didn't have a honeymoon, though, until after the war.

Rosemary Dawson remembers the christening of her brother in 1947 and what happened afterwards.
My brother Richard was born in 1947 when I was five and a half years old. He was christened in the Methodist church which was opposite our house in Pinner, north of London.

A few days later we were to have our photographs taken. We went to a real photographer's studio. I had to wear my party dress. It was made from shiny green material, and had a frill round the bottom, across my chest, round the puff sleeves and round the neck. I hated it. There was very little dress material in the shops, so my mother had made it out of an old bridesmaid's dress. I had a matching ribbon tied in a big bow in my hair. Richard was wearing his christening dress, which was long and lacy and had once been mine. He was put on a large soft cushion, on a table. I was told to stand behind, and gaze down at him while the picture was taken.

This was a family christening in 1943. Most of the men in the family were away fighting in the war, and so could not be at the christening.

Special Days 2

At the end of the war lots of people held street parties to celebrate victory. These children were from Brockley in south London.

Peggy George remembers how the end of the war was celebrated in Caerphilly.

At the end of the war in 1945 we had lots of celebrations on what was called VE day. VE stood for Victory in Europe. Nearly every street had a party for the children. All the neighbours brought out their dining tables and they were joined up in a long line in the street. Sheets were put over them like table cloths. The mothers made lots of sandwiches and jelly and blancmanges. There was still rationing, and so they had to be very inventive. Mostly the jellies were made from the orange juice that was supplied for babies. It was thickened with cornflour. I remember two women who lived with lots of children in a block of flats near us. They asked if they could join in. They came with a large metal bath filled with little cakes they had baked. We never did find out how they got hold of the flour and fat and sugar to make them!

Glossary

beret a round, flat, cloth cap.

box office a place where you buy tickets for the cinema or theatre

chink tiny crack that lets light through.

dammed blocked up.

decoded discovered the meaning.

evacuated moved to a safer place.

evacuee a person who is moved to a safer place.

fells and moors a stretch of hills and open land.

flares flames dropped from an aircraft to light up a target.

flex covered wires for carrying electricity.

halma a board game for two or four players.

holed a hole made in the side of the ship.

intercepted stopped something going from one place to another.

iron foundry a place where iron is melted down then hardened into different shapes.

kilner jars large glass jars with a tight lid.

mangle a machine which squeezes water out of wet clothes.

mined an area of ground where explosives have been buried.

oil refinery a place where oil is made pure and clean

pitchforked picked up and thrown using a two-pronged fork.

repertory performances of different plays by one company.

sea anemones a type of simple sea animal, like a brightly coloured jelly-fish.

scarce hard to find.

shells explosives that are fired from a big gun.

Spitfire an aeroplane used in World War 2.

stooks groups of wheatsheaves bunched together.

tig a chasing game, sometimes called 'he' or 'tag'.

wireless radio

Index